"If you like stories, you probably read a lot. And if you read this book, you will encounter a true life story about a man who loves to tell stories. This book is one story—about his life and faith. And it is many stories about his engagement with religion, the church, the Bible, sin and salvation, and his hope in God's love."

—Ezra Earl Jones, retired general secretary of the General Board of Discipleship of the United Methodist Church

"Not many people have the courage or take the time to share their life of faith with the world. John Covington, however, has done just that. In his own unique style, he takes the reader through the grand sweep of biblical tradition while sharing his own reactions to stories and characters many of us only heard about as children. Whether or not you agree with his interpretation, you will find the narrative engaging and thought-provoking. You might even learn a thing or two, and you are sure to get a chuckle out of some of John's antics. John Wesley encouraged Christians to go through life with the Bible in one hand and the newspaper in the other. I would suggest you use this heartfelt volume as a companion to your daily devotions."

—Rev. Dr. Penelope A. Gladwell, lead faculty, School of Leadership and Professional Development, Mountain State University

"John Covington has created a real gem in *Who is God and What am I Doing Here?*. He has an extraordinary ability to take the complex and make it simple. In the process, he makes the Bible and its teachings very approachable for all of us. John's honesty, humor and scholarship shine through every page. As you read this book, you will meet many fine people all with human needs just like ours. I particularly admire the honesty of Michelle, Leroy and the girl at the Maryland Department of Motor Vehicles. They were certainly blessed to meet John, and through this work, so are we."

—C. E. "Gus" Whalen Jr., chairman,
Warren Featherbone Communiversity,
Gainesville, Georgia. Author of four books;
the latest *Hooked at the Roots*

Who is God & What Am I Doing Here?

Who is God & What Am I Doing Here?

*A Quick
Guide to
Paradise*

John Covington

"Who is God & What Am I Doing Here?," by John Covington. ISBN 978-1-621379-744 (softcover).

Published 2017 by Virtualbookworm.com Publishing Inc., P.O. Box 9949, College Station, TX , 77842, US.

"Who is God and What Am I Doing Here?"

Acknowledgments

I would not be able to write a book if it was not for the many friends and colleagues that take the time to review my work, catch the spelling and grammatical errors, and also give wise content insight. I would like to thank and acknowledge Dr. Tom Berliner, Jeff Busts, Joe Closs, Leigh Covington, Reverend Jim Farmer, Dr. Penny Gladwell, Brad Newman, Jim Power, Reid Reininger, Mark Smith, Dr. Mike Umble, Jim Turbok, and Barbara Zinck. Without these great friends, this book would not be possible.

Table of Contents

Foreword

You are going to simply love this book—it does not matter if you are a longtime Christian or one looking for God in the midst of life. On every page you will find both God and self and find application for your current situation.

This is not an "ivory tower" theoretical treatise about God. Rather, John has filled these pages with encounters with the Living God.

In each chapter, John speaks straight to the heart, as well as the mind. We are delivered into the presence and work of God in the world in which we live. Spoken with simplicity and purity, John offers the reader a priceless treasure.

I heartily recommend this book. It is helpful and easy to read yet deep in meaning and purpose. Discipleship is important to John, and through these words, he offers the reader hope, encouragement, and, perhaps best of all, handles on which to take hold as we strive for purpose and direction in our lives.

John Covington is a man of success on many levels but none more so than as a man of faith. He shares the questions rather than giving us the answers far removed from our current struggle. He has confronted each of the questions himself and offers us the opportunity to take a Quick Guide to Paradise!

—Jim Farmer

Preface

When our daughter, Leigh, was in kindergarten, the mode of punishment for being mischievous was to "sit on the curb." Each day it was a big conversation between Leigh and my wife, Linda, about who sat on the curb that day and the associated offense. In kindergarten, being assigned to the curb was akin to a felony, and of course only the worst of the worst would be on the curb. It finally dawned on me that Leigh certainly had a lot of knowledge concerning those curb sitters. "Honey, do you ever have to sit on the curb?" I asked. "Oh, yes, Daddy, nearly every day." Poor Linda nearly had a heart attack to learn she had parented such a criminal and wondered where she had gone wrong. Sometimes asking an obvious question can change perspectives, and I have learned to do it as routine. That practice is the reason I feel moved to write this book.

Several years ago, I was talking with one of my coworkers, Michelle, during Easter, and out comes the question, "Michelle, do you know what all this Easter stuff is about?" At the time, Michelle was in her late thirties, married, and had three children. "Not really," she replied. "Do you want to know?" I asked. Michelle sat on the edge of her chair, looked me in the eye, and absorbed everything I said. For her, prior to that discussion, Easter was about chocolate, the bunny, and marshmallows. My natural follow-up question was, "So do you know why we celebrate Christmas?" and again, the answer was no.

I was taken aback. How can anyone live in the United States, be in their thirties, and not know why we celebrate Christmas and Easter?

Several weeks later, I went to get my driver's license renewed. The young lady who was administering my eye exam had a necklace with a cross. I commented on how I liked her cross. She said, "Oh, my grandmother gave me that because I am her only grandchild that goes to church." I said, "Well, that is nice. Where do you go?"

"I don't know the name, but they have really cool music. I'm not religious or anything," was her reply.

I am mentoring a man who was recently released from prison, and I bring him to Sunday school and church with me. In Sunday school, we were studying Isaiah in the Bible, and something was mentioned about being "delivered from evil." Leroy said, "That is what I need to pray for." I told him, "Well, each time you pray the Lord's Prayer, you will pray to be delivered from evil." Leroy asked, "What's the Lord's Prayer?"

When I leave for church each week, I pass by numerous houses where the parents do not go to church and their children stay at home with them. When those children are in their late thirties, will they know why we celebrate Easter and Christmas? I doubt it, or certainly not well.

However, not even church or synagogue attendance ensures a deep knowledge of who God is. Recently, I was having dinner with several friends and board members of a local charity. I was telling them about my project of writing this book during Lent, the time leading up to Easter, so a discussion of some of the biblical heroes ensued. Again, I was surprised at the lack of knowledge among several who are regular worshipers at either their church or synagogue.

The Apostles' Creed, Communion, Passover, Moses, John the Baptist, King David, the Bible, and even the Lord's Prayer are foreign terms to many. The Bible states folks are not going to learn if we do not tell them, so one of the reasons for writing this book is to attempt to do that.

Several years ago, I was doing some work for Crown Manufacturing in New Bremen, Ohio. At one time, there were no hotels in New Bremen, so folks would stay at one of the Crown properties. New Bremen is an old German farming community, and all of the places to stay are quaint, unique, and original buildings. On one trip, I stayed in the Queen Anne's house, which had been moved to the Crown property. In the house was a book describing life when the house was a home many years ago. Back then, most everything centered on a Christian lifestyle. Extra food was cooked on Saturday so the servants could have Sunday off with their family. Entertainment consisted of walks where Bible stories were told and discussed. That is not who we are today. The opportunity to learn about God is not as accessible as it was when it was part of the fabric of everyday life.

There has been a lot written about how we have grown further away from God as a nation. Whether you agree or disagree with no prayer in school or the near intolerance of a discussion about God in the public sector, that is our reality today. One of the natural results of this is that many people who would have normally been exposed to God in the public school system are not. Today, exposure to God is almost 100 percent up to parents. We have created an environment where getting to know God surely appears more difficult.

In this book, I am going to begin by seeking to answer the two questions the book's title asked and then try and build on that knowledge by eavesdropping on the discussion between the two men and the risen Jesus on their walk to the town of Emmaus. Over the course of the book, I hope to provide a general overview of the Bible. God reveals himself to us through his Holy Word, the Bible. Also, many everyday terms and holidays are biblically based, and you might enjoy learning more about them. I will point those out as we go along.

This book is not for the biblical scholar, although I plan to have a few review this before going to press. This book is for Michelle, Leroy, the girl at the Mary land Department of Motor Vehicles, and those like them that are curious to learn more about the world, the God who created our world, and why in the heck they exist on the planet. That might be important to them, so let's get going.

The Answer to the Two Questions

One either believes in God or they don't. If you believe God exists, then you see God everywhere. People see what they believe. If I believe you are smart, then I will see you doing smart things, which will validate my belief. If one truly believes in God, they see God in every detail of life. I believe in God. Do I have any supporting data? Yes, I think I do, but a lot of that happened between God and me. I will tell you some of my experiences and my logic, but I am not going to convince you, nor will I try. That is going to be between you and God.

My mother was a wonderful Christian lady. My dad died when I was six, and he did not have a lot of life insurance, so I guess we were "poor." I remember my mother working three jobs, one of which was teaching piano at our home. She was active in our church and made sure I went to worship service and Sunday school. In Sunday school, many of the lessons concerned great Bible stories, and they were in comic book format. I would roll up the books and hit the girls in the head with them. I think that was the beginning of the courting process for many young boys. I remember stories of Joseph, with his multicolored robe; Moses (who surely must have looked like Charlton Heston); and the shepherd David slaying the giant Goliath with a slingshot.

Most of us who believe in God can cite numerous stories about feeling God's presence, and I can also. I am only going to mention one for now. As a young boy, my favorite two possessions were a tattered baseball and a baseball bat. For hours I would stand in our backyard, throw the ball in the air, and swat it. I would imagine myself to be a star on the Washington Senators, and many times I would run around the backyard, circling the bases to the roar of the crowd after hitting a grand slam home run to win the game. Once in a while, I would hit the ball into the field next door, which was overgrown with weeds. My ball was essentially lost. What I would do is ask God to find my ball. I would then close my eyes, spin around, and release my bat into the field. The bat would always land next to the ball. What are the odds of that happening once, much less every time? That was a leap of faith on my part, as I could have also lost my bat. Not only was God looking out for my prized possession, he showed a little boy his presence and the importance of faith that would last a lifetime.

God is Creator of the universe; the One who made everything. How did God create the universe? Was it a big boom? Was it done in seven days, as we know them today? Did we evolve from apes? Heck, I don't know, but guess what—no one else does either. I am a chemical engineer by training, so I have studied a lot more science than most, and I am not overly awed by scientists; all of them think they are right. The only thing I am convinced of is that scientists will continue to argue about it for the rest of my lifetime, and it really doesn't matter to me. I figure I will have my time to ask God directly. I have bigger fish to fry during my relatively short span on earth.

Even though many people do not know a lot about God, surveys show that a vast majority believes in his existence. I believe there is a God, that he created the universe, and that the Bible is the living Word of God that he inspired men to write. I do not complicate my belief system with much more than that.

Let's talk a little about us. Have you noticed that people are different from the rest of the animals? I know it seems obvious. Did you also notice that people can really be a pain in the neck? At times, people start wars, pollute the environment, abuse their children, treat each other unfairly, and are unfaithful. Other than that, people are just great to have around. So the same God that made dogs—a wonderful animal that gives unconditional love and wags its tail for you—also created this obnoxious thing called a human. Why? Why would God create such a monster?

The answer is that he wanted someone to love and worship him. It is that simple; God wanted to have children, so he made us in his own image.

Now you can start being logical. If God made us to love and worship him, then he must give us freedom of choice—free will. It would not be fair if God made us to love him and then turned around and made it so we have no choice; that would not be love, so we must have a choice. And if God gives us free will, then we can choose to do what is right or wrong. Therefore, we are sometimes going to choose what is wrong and harm the relationship between God and us.

The first man was Adam, and according to the Bible, God made the first woman from Adam's rib. I do not know how this happened, but if God said he made Eve from a rib, then so be it. I am not going to lose sleep over it. Adam and Eve were created in the garden of Eden. This is a real place, by the way. Many historians believe that the garden of Eden was located somewhere in Iraq. Everything in the garden was set up pretty good—plenty of food to eat, and Adam and Eve enjoyed each other's company. Adam said of Eve:

> The man said, 'This is now bone of my bones and flesh of my flesh; she shall be called woman, for she was taken out of man.' For this reason a man will leave his father and mother and be united to his wife and they will become one flesh. The man and his wife were both naked and felt no shame.
>
> Genesis 2:23-25 (niv)

God also told them they could eat from any tree, except the tree of knowledge.

Let us pause here for a second. We have Adam and Eve in a beautiful garden, with plenty to eat, communing with God, and running around naked becoming one flesh, and no one cares. Can life get much better than that? Only one instruction: do not eat from the tree of knowledge.

This is where a pinch of human nature kicks in. I do not know about you, but when someone tells me not to do something, a little thing in my system starts to figure out how to do it. That is true even today. My wife, Linda, says, "Do not leave the lid up on the toilet!" That is the best way to ensure I will leave the lid up; the only variable is how much grief I want to endure.

The devil came to Adam and Eve in the form of a serpent and began to explain to them logically why they should eat from the tree of knowledge, and he was successful. After they had eaten from the tree, they hid from God and covered their bodies with fig leafs. God knew immediately what they had done, and our troubles began. Adam and Eve messed it up for us. However, you and I would have done the same thing. When you hear people talk about "the original sin," this was it. Eve and Adam ate from the tree of knowledge when God had specifically forbidden them to eat that fruit. They knowingly disobeyed.

The issue now is that humans have sinned against God and the relationship is strained. When we sin, we always offend God, and some of God's other children are harmed. We normally do not commit a sin and fail to harm someone in the act. When we do a bad thing, others are hurt. Let's say someone cheats on his or her spouse. How many people are harmed by that sin? Of course the spouse is hurt. In addition, there are children, friends, and many others. Anything we do impacts others, so when we do something bad, we impact them in a negative manner. In order to reconcile our relationship with God, he sent Jesus, who was God in human form, to pay for our sins by being beaten, whipped, and nailed through his hands and feet to a cross until he died.

Things went from bad to worse in the garden of Eden to the point where God kicked them out of the garden. They had children, and the human race began to multiply. The first two children they had were Cain and Abel. It also only took one generation of humans to have our first murder. Cain was jealous of Abel. Both young men had brought gifts to God, and Abel had put out more effort, so God praised his gifts. Cain got angry and murdered his brother. When God asked Cain where Abel was,

Cain replied, "I don't know. Am I my brother's keeper?" (Genesis 4:9b, niv) You may have heard that term before—now you know the origin.

As hundreds of years went by, humans became worse, ignoring God and not obeying him. God finally got fed up and flooded the planet. The only one who survived was our good friend Noah and his family. God had come to Noah and told him to build this mammoth ark (big ship). Put yourself in Noah's shoes; would you have gone out and dedicated a good portion of your life to do this construction when all the skies are sunny and your neighbors are laughing at you? Well, thank heaven Noah did, and he got a pair of each type of animal to put in the ark with him. The waters of the flood receded, and God gave the sign of the rainbow. The rainbow was God's covenant with Noah that never again would he destroy the world by water. So the next time you see a rainbow, you will know it is a sign of one of God's covenants.

Again, after many generations, Noah's descendants were spread all over the world and had formed different nations. There came a time that all of these nations decided to build a huge tower that would reach all the way to heaven so they could make a name for themselves. The Lord foiled their plan by changing their languages: "Come, let us go down and confuse their language so they will not understand each other" (Genesis 11:7, niv). The tower they were building was the Tower of Babel, and I am sure you have heard the expression of "people babbling." So now you know where all that comes from.

God was struggling with the people he had created to love and worship him. The vast majority of these folks were only concerned with taking care of their own selfish wishes. God then began to implement his next plan. He selected one group upon which to focus as his "chosen people," his "light unto the world." His devotion to them would enable the rest of the world to see God's greatness. God chose Abraham, a fellow living in what is now Iraq, whom God made the father of a new nation of Hebrew (Jewish) people living in present-day Israel. God had chosen to focus on the Jewish people.

Who is God? That is a heck of a question. The God that a large portion of the world worships is the God of Abraham. Jews, Christians, and Muslims worship the God of Abraham. Muslims refer to him as Allah, Jews call him El Shaddi, and Christians call him God—three in one (Father, Son, and Holy Spirit).

Abraham and his wife, Sarah, were old and did not have any children. Sarah had Abraham sleep with her Egyptian handmaiden, Hagar, which was the custom back then when a wife was barren. Hagar bore Abraham a son, Ishmael. Then an angel of the Lord came to Sarah and Abraham and told them they would have a natural child by Sarah. Sarah thought that was so crazy, she laughed, which got her in some trouble with the angel. Sarah bore Abraham a son, Isaac. The Bible focuses on Isaac as the natural son of Abraham, and it is from his descendants that he makes his covenant with his chosen people. Muslims embrace the theory that Ishmael is the number one son, so the conflict between Jews and Muslims goes back that far.

Isaac had two sons, Jacob and Esau. The Jews and Christians embrace Jacob, and the Muslims embrace Esau. Many Jews and Christians refer to God as the God of Abraham, Isaac, and Jacob.

I am a Christian, so you will get the Christian view point from all of this.

Christians see God as the Trinity: the Father, the Son, and the Holy Spirit. A lot of people make this more complicated than need be. Jesus is God incarnate, which means God in the flesh. God came to earth in human form to live with us and to be a sacrifice for our sins. His death on the cross was the sacrifice, and his resurrection three days later at Easter was our victory over death. The verse you see in the stands of many athletic events is John 3:16-17 (niv), which is: "For God so loved the world that he gave his one and only Son, that whoever believes in Him shall not perish but have eternal life. For God did not send his Son into the world to condemn the world, but to save the world through him." Before Christ left the world, he told his disciples he would leave them with the Holy Spirit. The Holy Spirit is Christ dwelling in them and also in us.

A prayer by Reverend Beverly Jones reads: "O God, our refuge and our strength, lead us into the truth of Christ, that whatever befalls us this day will be a reminder of him in whom you dwell and through whom you dwell in us. Amen" (Upper Room Disciplines, 2010, page 64).

That prayer describes the God Christians worship.

God is our creator, refuge, and strength—the "Daddy figure." Christ intercedes for us and shows us how to live, the friend, mentor, and advocate figure, and the Holy Spirit (that which dwells in us) is God with and talking with us.

Here are some descriptions of God that our pastor handed out with supporting Bible verses:

- Creator, "In the beginning, when God created the heavens and the earth, the earth was a formless void and darkness covered the face of the deep while a wind from God swept over the face of the waters" (Genesis 1:12, niv).
- God Almighty, "Then I heard what seemed to be the voice of a great multitude, like the sound of many waters and like the sound of mighty thunder peals, crying out, 'Hallelujah! For the Lord our God the Almighty reigns'" (Revelation 19:6, niv).
- My Shepherd, "The Lord is my shepherd, I shall not want" (Psalm 23:1, niv).
- Mother, "As a mother comforts her child, so I will comfort you; you shall be com forted in Jerusalem" (Isaiah 66:13, niv).
- Advocate, "But the Advocate, the Holy Spirit, whom the Father will send in my name, will teach you everything, and remind you of all that I have said to you" (John 14:26, niv).
- God of Peace, "The God of peace be with all of you" (Romans 15:33, niv).

We are now going to transition from whom God is. I am going to assume that since you are reading this you want to learn something about God and his history with us.

The Walk to Emmaus

To learn more about God, we are going to start by eavesdropping on a couple of fellows walking to Emmaus about two thousand years ago. We begin our journey of learning about God on the most holy day of all, Easter; in fact, the first Easter. Jesus was crucified on Friday and buried in a tomb before Friday evening, which begins the Jewish Sabbath. The authorities wanted to get him off the cross and into a grave before the beginning of Sabbath. The two men walking to Emmaus must have had a lot on their mind, as so much had happened. They were followers of Christ, so they were saddened by the weekend events. As they were walking, Jesus (who was supposed to be dead) joined them. Here is the story as related by Luke:

> Now that same day, two of them were going to a village called Emmaus, about seven miles from Jerusalem. They were talking with each other about everything that had happened. As they talked and discussed these things with each other, Jesus himself came up and walked along with them; but they were kept from recognizing Him. He asked them, "What are you discussing together as you walk along?" They stood still, their faces downcast. One of them, named Cleopas, asked him, "Are you the only one living in Jerusalem who doesn't know the things that have happened there in these days?" "What things," he asked. "About Jesus of Nazareth," they replied. "He was a prophet, powerful in word and deed before God

and all the people. The chief priests and our rulers handed him over to be sentenced to death, and they crucified him; but we had hoped that he was the one who was going to redeem Israel. And what is more, it is the third day since all this took place. In addition, some of our women amazed us. They went to the tomb early this morning but didn't find his body. They came and told us that they had seen a vision of angels, who said he was alive. Then some of our companions went to the tomb and found it just as the women had said, but him they did not see." He said to them, "How foolish you are, and how slow of heart to believe all that the prophets have spoken! Did not the Christ have to suffer these things and then enter his glory?" And beginning with Moses and all the Prophets, he explained to them what was said in all the Scriptures concerning himself. As they approached the village to which they were going, Jesus acted as if he were going further. But they urged him strongly, "Stay with us, for it is nearly evening; the day is almost over." So he went in to stay with them. When he was at the table with them, he took bread, gave thanks, broke it, and began to give it to them. Then their eyes were opened and they recognized him and he disappeared from their sight. They asked each other, "Were not our hearts burning within us while he talked with us on the road and opened the Scriptures to us?" They got up and returned at once to Jerusalem. There they found the eleven and those with them assembled together and saying, "It is true! The Lord has risen and has appeared to Simon." Then the two told what had happened on the way, and how Jesus was recognized by them when he broke the bread.

Luke 24:13-35 (niv)

Let us flash back a few weeks and recall what went on in Jerusalem.

Jesus was in his mid-thirties and had a huge following. Many of the Jews hoped he was the Messiah God had promised. God had told his people about the Messiah through his prophets. The Messiah was to deliver the Jews from persecution and establish God's kingdom on earth so that the house of David would again rule over the Jewish people. Many of the Jews thought the Messiah would come in the form of a military king. Judas, who would later betray Christ, was such a person.

The popularity of Jesus upset the Hebrew priests, and they had plotted for years on ways to rid themselves of him. At the time, Israel was ruled by the Romans, so getting Jesus in trouble with the Romans would be one way to solve the problem of Jesus. The story of Easter week begins on the previous Sunday, what we refer to today as Palm Sunday.

On Palm Sunday, Jesus rode atop a donkey into the city. (For hundreds of years, this was the action of Jewish kings, and Jewish prophets predicted the Messiah would do this too.) His followers and admirers waved palm branches and threw them down in the path of the donkey. The Jewish people were all coming to Jerusalem to celebrate Passover, one of their most holy holidays. With the people making such a fuss over Jesus, the Jewish leaders got even angrier.

In our church, we celebrate Palm Sunday by giving everyone in the congregation palm branches. These branches are later collected, burned, and the ashes are used for the next year's "Ash Wednesday" service, which signifies the beginning of Lent. Lent is a time of self-reflection and sacrifice forty days before Easter in memory of Jesus going without food and drink for forty days in the desert. You may hear about people giving up something like chocolate for Lent as a form of sacrifice. By the way, Mardi Gras is the celebration before Lent where everyone parties and gets it out of their system. Although New Orleans gets most of the publicity for Mardi Gras, Mobile, Alabama, claims to have conducted the first Mardi Gras. As you can see, a lot of holidays and special events today are centered on Christ coming to Jerusalem to fulfill his mission.

During Passover, the Jews celebrate their escape from Egypt. Let's talk about that and then rejoin Jesus and his disciples, as they will celebrate Passover together in the upper room.

Passover and Communion

As I mentioned, Passover is when the Jews celebrate their escape from Egypt thousands of years ago. One might ask, "What in the heck were they doing there to start with?" Let's find out.

Isaac's son Jacob, whom we discussed in the previous chapter, had twelve sons. Jacob's favorite son was Joseph. I know we are not supposed to have favorites. One of the many things I like about Bible stories is that the people in these stories are like you and me; they are messed up. Jacob was not too subtle on how much more he liked Joseph and his younger brother, Benjamin. As sign of his love, Jacob gave Joseph a beautiful robe of many colors.

One day while the older sons were out in the field tending the flocks, Jacob asked Joseph to go check on them. Now the brothers disliked Joseph because their father favored him so much. So when they saw him coming, they made plans to kill him. Cooler heads prevailed, and instead of killing him, they sold him to a group of merchants who later sold him into slavery in Egypt. Then they went back and told their father, Jacob, that Joseph had been killed by wild animals.

While in Egypt, Joseph was a model prisoner and was given a lot of responsibility. He eventually rose to be a high-ranking officer and Pharaoh (the ruler of Egypt) trusted him. Not only was he no longer a prisoner, but he was also one of the highest-ranking officials in all of Egypt.

During this period, Jacob and his family, who were still in Israel, found themselves in the midst of a famine. They heard Egypt had plenty of extra grain, so Jacob sent his sons to Egypt with many fine gifts to swap for grain so they would not starve. Can you imagine their surprise when the older brothers discovered Joseph was responsible for allocating the Egyptian grain? I am sure they were initially afraid that Joseph would want revenge and harm them. However, all Joseph wanted was to be reunited with his family and to see his father and younger brother, Benjamin, so he sent his brothers back to retrieve them.

As a result of the famine, many of the Hebrew people came to Egypt for the grain and stayed many generations. Eventually, the Hebrew people who were slaves in Egypt grew in population, and many of the Egyptians were afraid of them. Numerous generations had passed, and Joseph and Jacob had been dead for a long time, along with their happy memories. The Hebrew people were being abused to the point that many of their male babies were being killed. During one of those killing sprees, a Hebrew mother took her newborn son, put him in a basket, and floated him down the Nile in the hopes he would be rescued. One of Pharaoh's daughters found the baby and raised it as her own. She named the baby Moses.

Moses is one of the big characters in the Bible and holds a place of esteem along with Abraham and King David (the fellow that took out the giant Goliath with a slingshot). God had a special role for Moses, and that was to deliver his people out of slavery in Egypt into the Promised Land, which is present-day Israel. When God first came to Moses, he balked at the task, citing he was not qualified. After a mild debate with God, Moses— assisted by his brother, Aaron—took on the challenge.

Many times, God uses unlikely people to carry out his plan—people like Moses, you, the disciples, and me.

Moses went to the pharaoh, seeking to negotiate the freedom of his people. Those negotiations did not go well, even when God gave Pharaoh several signs in the form of plagues, such as water turning to blood and a bunch of frogs running around everywhere. What finally got Pharaoh's attention was a plague of death of the firstborn males in all of Egypt, from the firstborn son of Pharaoh to cattle.

God had the Hebrew people smear some goat or lamb's blood on their doorposts to indicate they were Hebrew. The angel of death, who was to kill the firstborn males, would "pass over" those houses, and they would be spared—hence the term Passover. Also, that evening of the Passover, they were to have a feast on lamb or goat, bitter herbs, and bread made without yeast.

The meat was to be drained of blood and was to be roasted. This is where the ideas behind kosher food come from. The Passover meal the Hebrew people celebrated is, to this day, referred to as a Seder meal. Your Jewish friends still have a Seder meal to celebrate Passover. Passover is one of the most holy days in the Jewish calendar.

Many feel the "Last Supper" that Christ shared with his disciples in the upper room was a Passover Seder meal. This particular meal was on the night before Jesus was crucified. During that Last Supper, Christ took bread and said, "Take and eat; this is my body." Then he took the cup of wine, gave thanks, and offered it to them, saying, "Drink from it, all of you. This is my blood of the covenant, which is poured out for many for the forgiveness of sins" (Matthew 26:26b-28, niv)

When Christians take Communion, the bread represents the body of Christ, and the wine, or grape juice, rep resents the blood of Christ. Catholics and some Protestants take real wine at Communion, but most Protestants take grape juice. I am a United Methodist. Methodists used to be big in the Prohibition movement, so alcohol was not tolerated. A Methodist by the name of Dr. Welch came up with a way of pasteurizing grape juice so it could be used for Communion, and that was the beginning of Welch's grape juice and the company that produced it. So the next time you are in the juice section of the grocery store, you can think about Holy Communion.

For many centuries, Christians and Jews did not get along. Most Christians ignored their Jewish origins and expanded to include non-Jewish. Jesus was a Jew, and Jewish customs were his customs; therefore, many of them are ours. Fortunately, both faiths have grown in maturity, and many Christians have even embraced some of the traditions, such as having a Seder meal at Passover. Today, some of Israel's most avid supporters are Christians from the United States.

There are two main groups of Christians: Catholics and Protestants. In my opinion, there is little difference in theology between the two. They all used to believe the other group was going straight to hell when they died. Perhaps some on both sides still believe that, but the rank and file doesn't. The only two differences I see concern Mary, the mother of Jesus, and the concept of Communion. Protestants believe that only Jesus "ascended" into heaven, but Catholics believe that Mary also ascended into heaven. Also, Catholics believe that the bread and wine at Communion are actually the body and blood of Christ, whereas most Protestants believe they only represent the body and blood. Other than that, I do not see a dime's worth of difference, other than the status given to certain religious leaders, such as the pope.

Unfortunately, many of history's worst conflicts have been over religion, and today, we are not far removed from that violence. An example is the conflict in Northern Ireland between Protestants and Catholics. It is absolutely absurd that these two groups would fight to exterminate the other. For centuries in Europe, there were bloody massacres between Protestants and Catholics and, in Europe and the Middle East, wars between Muslims and Christians. I remember as a child that there was strain between Catholics and Protestants in the United States. When John Kennedy, who was Catholic, was running for president, many were concerned that the pope would end up running the country. I once dated a Catholic girl, and my mother had a fit. That was just not done back then. By the way, I am sure her parents were not all that thrilled either.

Who Am I?

When God was talking to Abraham, he told him that his descendants would be more numerous than the stars in the sky. Another phrase I have heard when talking about people is that we are more numerous than specks of sand on the earth.

Most of us live fewer than a hundred years. In the grand scheme of things, that is a small dot compared to God's time frame of thousands of years. Are you feeling small and insignificant yet? Well, you should. You are one of a bazillion specks of sand, and you are only going to be around for a wisp of time, then you will be gone, never to be remembered again, except by a few close relatives, and when they die off, there will be no one who will remember you or your life. We are not Abraham Lincoln; we will not have a monument named after us.

If I look at my existence through the eyes of an atheist or using logic, then it is sort of dismal. But if I look at my life as being special with responsibility and a job to do, then I feel a lot better about things.

So here is what is amazing to me: You and I are children of God, and he knows each of us.

> Before I formed you in the womb I knew you, before you were born I set you apart; I appointed you as a prophet to the nations.
>
> Jeremiah 1:5 (niv)

Just try to grasp this: A bazillion people have lived or are living for just a wisp of time, but God has a special place in his heart and a special plan for each one of us. The only variable is whether or not we reach out and go after it. It is almost impossible to comprehend; all the folks in China, India, Africa—all the continents since the beginning of time—are special to God. How in the heck does he keep track of it all?

> You did not choose me, but I chose you to go and bear fruit—fruit that will last. Then the Father will give you whatever you ask in my name. This is my command: Love one another.
>
> John 15:16-17 (niv)

Jesus is telling his followers that he has chosen them, and he wants them to go out and do something good. His simple command of "love one another" would translate into many good things, if we were to do it.

I read a devotional written by a prison chaplain. The chaplain was ministering to a death row inmate who was nearing execution. The chaplain told the man that he was a child of God. The condemned man perked up and said, "I have been called many things in my life, but never a child of God."

"Who am I?" One of the answers to this question is that you are a child of God who is loved by God more than your parents love you or more than you love your own children. That is who you are.

You are also a person with a freedom of choice. Unlike the other animals on the planet that behave mostly by instinct, you can choose your behavior. Therein lays a huge problem for us. Most of us learn how early choices affect the options we have later. I remember talking to Nichole, the daughter of one of my wife's cousins. At the time, Nichole was a crazy teenager and was being pretty rebellious, as many teens are. She was getting awful grades, staying in trouble, and pretty much mad at the world. I still remember the scowl on her face as she slumped down in a chair in our den. "Nichole, do you like people telling you what you can do?" I asked. Of course the answer was a resounding no. I tried to explain that choices she made now with respect to studying, etc., would impact the level of choices she had down the road. Nichole now lives a life of people telling her what to do: she is in prison, and she has been in and out of prison numerous times. Until Nichole makes some different choices in her life, I do not see a lot of hope for her. Nichole, like many, is in danger of living a life of unfulfilled potential. But it is her choice.

> Steve Barse, writing for *Disciplines*, says:
> I think God has a purpose for all of us. That purpose is not unlike goal posts on a football field. Between the two goal posts exists God's good and perfect will. When we aim to stay within those posts, we find happiness, security, wellbeing, joy, peace and the freedom to be who God intends us to be. To live outside these goal posts opens us up to every manner of distress, fear, and harm.
>
> Disciplines, 2010, pg. 81

We are free to choose how we respond to God's love. If we choose to love God and other people, we feel as though we are part of a larger community and life can be a lot of fun.

As I am writing this chapter, Michelle and I (yep, the same Michelle that was struggling with Easter) just returned from Sherod Cooper's funeral. Sherod is the brother of Liz, our controller, and Michelle and I went to pay our respects. The church was packed with Sherod's friends and family. They had to bring out folding chairs. I did not know Sherod other than he has a mighty fine sister. I do not know anything about his beliefs; however, since the ceremony included several hymns and scripture readings, I am going to make the assumption that he was a believer. One of the passages is comforting and is read at many funerals. It is a passage that makes us not feel so small:

"Do not let your hearts be troubled. Believe in God, believe also in me. In my Father's house there are many dwelling places. If it were not so, I would have told you. I am going there to prepare a place for you. And if I go and prepare a place for you, I will come back and take you to be with me that you may be where I am. You know the way to the place where I am going." Thomas said to him, "Lord, we don't know where you are going, so how can we know the way?" Jesus answered, "I am the way and the truth and the life. No one comes to the Father except through me."

John 14:16 (niv)

Jesus has prepared a place for each of his believers to dwell. Pretty comforting thought after being made to feel so insignificant.

Sherod's ceremony began with the singing of "Amazing Grace," a hymn that most everyone has heard and knows. I whispered to Michelle during the service that the hymn was written by a reformed slave trader. She said, "You need to put that in the book!" So here it is.

Linda and I recently went to the funeral of a dear Jewish friend, Marlene Stirmer, and it was a contrast from the one we attended for Sherod. Marlene; her husband, Joe; and their sons, Billy and Lloyd, are close friends.

Jews normally bury the dead within two days; however, Marlene died on Friday morning, which was too close to the Jewish Sabbath (Friday evening to Saturday evening), so they buried her on Sunday.

When we entered the service area, a rabbi was reading out loud in Hebrew. Once the service began, there was the reading of Psalm 23, a rabbi spoke briefly, and then four people gave tributes to Marlene. Psalm 23 is one that is famous enough to quote. Many memorized this particular Psalm in the King James translation of the Bible (the really old one), and, to me, it would sound silly in any other version. King David is given the credit for writing Psalm 23:

> The Lord is my shepherd; I shall not want. He maketh me to lie down in green pastures: he leadeth me beside the still waters. He restoreth my soul: he leadeth me in the paths of righteousness for his name's sake. Yea, though I walk through the valley of the shadow of death, I will fear no evil: for thou art with me; thy rod and thy staff they comfort me. Thou preparest a table before me in the presence of mine enemies: thou anointest my head with oil; my cup runneth over. Surely goodness and mercy shall follow me all the days of my lie: and I will dwell in the house of the Lord forever.
>
> Psalm 23 (kjv)

Again, think how God is the shepherd for each of us, and it is amazing considering how many of us there are.

We then went to the cemetery, where there was a brief service and prayer. I noticed that there was a big pile of dirt and two shovels sitting by the gravesite. I initially thought, Well, that is pretty tacky. Don't the folks running this cemetery have enough compassion to do a better job? However, after the ending prayer, people lined up to shovel dirt upon Marlene's coffin, so Linda and I joined in and also shoveled dirt. Billy Stirmer met us on the way to our car and said, "I hope you threw some dirt on Mom's grave, because that is the biggest tribute you can give to a Jewish person, as it lasts forever." Billy then told Linda and me that he had tossed on twenty-one shovels of dirt, because each time he left his mom, she would kiss him twenty one times. Linda and I left thinking that we would like to have a Christian funeral with a Jewish twist to it. It was the best funeral I have ever attended.

Was your life an accident? Did your parents have one too many one evening, and all of a sudden, "Whoops, I'm pregnant" was the result?

I was born in 1948, and my mother was over forty years old. At that time, it was just taken for granted that women who got pregnant at that age would not be able to have a successful childbirth. In fact, my mother did not know she was pregnant until she was pretty well down the path of having a baby. I guess she just figured the Roanoke water system was having a couple of bad months and she needed to cut back on the pasta and meat sauce. Even when she went to the hospital, it was again taken for granted that I would not be born alive or make it home. It was a big shock to everyone that Mom and Dad were now Mom and Dad, and someone had better start thinking about diapers and all of the other stuff that comes along with babies. It was pretty obvious that I was not "planned" by Mom and Dad but perhaps planned by God. God gave Mom and Dad the responsibility of caring for his child (me). And it is the same with us all.

I imagine being hit unexpectedly with a kid when you are in your forties was a big deal and a change. Mom loved to tell the story of one of her first major snafus. She was out putting clothes on the laundry line, and Dad was outside painting. Mother carried her wet laundry in a long white metal container, which was perfect for a toddler to sit in. Somehow, I had gotten Dad's turpentine, got the lid off the bottle, and poured it in the tub where I was sitting. When Mom arrived on the scene, I was having a blast; however, my rubber pants were coming apart, and there was a rash around my mouth. Mom went into full-bore panic, and she and the neighbor lady swooped me down to the local country doctor. Poor Dad was probably left with his mouth gaping open. Old Doctor Jones quickly determined that I was going to make it, in spite of my mother. "Mildred, you are just going to have to pay more attention," was his advice.

When I use my human logic to consider those grains of sand and eons of time mentioned earlier in the chapter, I am made to feel insignificant. However, the Word of God tells us otherwise. Psalm 139, another psalm written by King David, reads:

> O Lord, you have searched me and you know me. You know when I sit and when I rise; you perceive my thoughts from afar. You discern my going out and my lying down; you are familiar with all my ways. Before a word is on my tongue you know it completely, O Lord. You hem me in—behind and before; you have laid your hand upon me. Such knowledge is too wonderful for me, too lofty for me to attain. Where can I go from your Spirit? Where can I flee from your presence? If I go up to the heavens, you are there; if I make my bed in the depths, you are there. If I rise on the wings of the dawn, if I settle on the far side of the sea, even there your hand will hold me fast. If I say "Surely the darkness will hide me and the light become night around me," even the darkness will not be dark to you the night will shine like the day, for darkness is as light to you.
>
> Psalm 139:1-12 (niv)

We are not ignored by God; we are actually wooed and stalked by God. King David laments he cannot get away from God. We had a pastor one time that said, "God even goes to the bathroom with you." Yuck—that is just more information than I need.

The point is even though a bazillion of us may live throughout time, we are all special.

What Am I Doing Here?

In addition to loving and worshiping God, we are supposed to work, serve others, and fulfill God's purpose for our lives. That is what we are doing here. We have a God given purpose, and it evolves until we die. On the way to work one morning, I was listening to an interview with Franklin Graham, the son of Billy Graham. The interviewer asked how Franklin's dad was doing, and Franklin said he was doing great and still working at ninety-one but with not as much energy. Billy Graham is currently redoing one of his books based on things that he has learned since he first published it. The interviewer said it was remarkable that even Billy Graham is constantly learning about and evolving in God's plan and work.

Many Christians feel that Pastor Rick Warren, author of the best seller The Purpose Driven Life, is the heir apparent to Billy Graham as the world's most influential Christian spiritual leader, along with the pope. On the cover flap of his book, Pastor Warren writes:

> You are not an accident. Even before the universe was created, God had you in mind, and he planned you for his purposes. These purposes will extend far beyond the few years you will spend on earth. You were made to last forever! Knowing God's purpose for creating you will reduce your stress, focus your

energy, simplify your decisions, give meaning to your life, and most important; prepare you for eternity.

Several years after my dad died, my mother started dating. My mom was an attractive lady, even in her late forties, and there were plenty of suitors. We lived in Oakton, Virginia, which was a rural community between Fairfax and Vienna.

I remember two suitors in particular. One fellow showed up in a suit all the time, and I think he was a telephone company executive. It was obvious to me that I was in the way and he would be happy if I were not in the picture. They would go on dates, and I would entertain myself while they were gone. Those were different times, and it was okay. Besides, if anything happened, I just had to run about twenty yards to the Atkinson family next door. I must have been about nine at the time.

I was an avid fisherman, and my tackle box was an old, plastic bandage container. This executive suitor promised to get me a tackle box, and I was excited. I think he said that just to impress my mom, because I never got the tackle box. The second fellow was Ray Carswell. Ray had been divorced several times (big nono back then), lived in Maryland (a foreign Yankee country), and worked at the government printing office as a union printer. On his first date, he brought me a Roy Seivers baseball bat (Roy was the star ball player for the Senators) and went out and played catch with me. When he and Mom were getting ready to leave on their date, I was seated on our sofa, ready to settle in for an evening of entertaining myself, when Ray said, "Boy, if you are going with us, you had best get ready!" I was ready in a flash.

One day, my Mom sat me down for a serious talk. It was almost like the talk we had when she told me my Dad had died and would not be coming home from work. The topic of this talk, however, was the next dad, as both men had proposed to my mom. She asked me to make the decision. Are you kidding me? I am going to make this decision? I said "Ray Carswell" so fast, it would make your head spin.

I remember their wedding, and I also remember being irritated because I was not invited on the honeymoon. Later, I came to understand why.

Our new family sold the property in Oakton and moved to Springfield, Virginia, which was a booming new community closer to Washington and Ray's work at the printing office. I was in the sixth grade and was a "little country" compared to some of the other kids. Many of our neighbors were wealthier than us, but Ray made a decent salary, and my mom could squeeze a nickel until the buffalo screamed, so we survived. Many of the folks in Springfield were college educated, which was not the case in Oakton. Soon there became a feeling that I would go to college; it was just an attitude that seemed to develop. Looking back in time, I know that Mom and Ray would not have been able to afford to send me to college, but it was just a "given" that I was going. I ended up doing okay in high school and earned an appointment to the US Naval Academy (where I did not have to pay), so off to college I went. And from there, I have bumbled to where I am today in life.

However, this little discussion is not about me. It is about Ray Crumpton Carswell; he changed the course of my life. Or was it God who changed the course of my life and he worked through Ray Carswell? My mom and I also changed Ray's life.

No father could have loved me any more than Ray, and his extended family of brothers, sisters, and other relatives became our family. As of today, Ray has been deceased well over three decades and is buried in Mobile, Alabama, along with my mom. Some of the children of his sisters and brother (my cousins) and their children are friends of my family today.

Ray stayed at home when Mom and I would go to church, except on special occasions, such as Easter and Christmas. On occasion, Ray drank more than he should. Both Mom and Ray had many health problems, and we spent many hours and days in hospital waiting rooms awaiting the outcome of serious operations. That may have been the only time Ray prayed, although I will hasten to add that I do not know the relationship Ray had with God.

How would my life have turned out if Mom had not married Ray? Would I have met my wife and thus been father to my daughter? I could go on, as could we all on a topic like this. How many other lives did Ray impact before me?

We can pick any human being and consider their life and the enormous impact they have on others and on the world. Pick someone in your life and ponder the impact. The people that have impacted my life are too numerous to count. Each day, loved ones and strangers are touching us.

Each of us impacts the world—sometimes for good and sometimes for bad. As God uses each of us for his plan, so does the devil. Adolf Hitler is probably one of the most infamous leaders in history. Like the Islamic terrorist of today, Hitler wrapped his evil in a blanket of godly righteousness.

There has been a lot written about God's purpose for your life, and I will not try and duplicate any of that.

I reviewed this book project with Milton Nettles, an outstanding chemical engineering student at the University of Alabama. Milton suggested I include Ephesians 2:10 (niv), which reads, "For we are God's workmanship, created in Christ Jesus to do good works, which God pre pared in advance for us to do." It certainly helps answer the question, "What am I doing here?"

Who is King David?

Another big player in God's love story is King David. Through the prophets, God told us in the Bible that the Messiah would come from the seed of King David. If you ever fly first class on the Israeli air carrier El Al, you will be in the King David section. King David is right up there with Moses and Abraham with respect to key people in the Old Testament of the Bible. The Old Testament is what we Christians call all of the books written before Christ, and the Jews embrace it as their holy scriptures also. The New Testament focuses on Christ and the beginnings of the Christian Church. Christians believe in both as the Word of God, and that is why our Bible contains both the Old and the New Testaments.

Jesus came from the genealogy of King David. For a long time, the Hebrew people did not have a king. They seemed to get along with religious leaders and whatever leader or prophet God seemed to have looking after them at the time. However, since all of the other nations surrounding them had a king, they wanted one also. God took this as a rejection of his leadership but basically said, "Hey, if you want a king, we will get you a king." The first king anointed was King Saul. King Saul did a pretty good job for a while, but then that old ego thing started getting in the way, and he became a jerk. God gets irritated at jerks, so he made the decision to get rid of Saul as king and appoint another one. Samuel was the prophet God was working through at the time, so he instructed Samuel to go to Bethlehem to a guy named Jesse, and one of his sons would be the next king. Jesse's youngest son, David, was the one God chose to be the next king.

"He was ruddy, with a fine appearance and handsome features" (1 Samuel 16:12b, niv)

David was actually the king-in-waiting because Saul was still the king. David became Saul's harp player. David was certainly well rounded: he was a musician, shepherd, and he was also a great warrior and writer of many of the psalms.

The Hebrew people stayed at war with the Philistines, and the time of young David was no exception. The Philistines had a massive champion named Goliath. Goliath was over nine feet tall and was a mighty warrior. What happened next is told in Samuel 17:8-11 (niv):

> Goliath stood and shouted to the ranks of Israel, "Why do you come out and line up for battle? Am I not a Philistine, and are you not the servants of Saul? Choose a man and have him come down to me. If he is able to fight and kill me, we will become your subjects; but if I overcome him and kill him, you will become our subjects and serve us." Then the Philistine said, "This day I defy the ranks of Israel! Give me a man and let us fight each other." On hearing the Philistine's words, Saul and all the Israelites were dismayed and terrified.

Of all people, David, still a young shepherd boy, came forward to fight Goliath. David was confident that the Lord was with him, and he convinced Saul to let him fight the Philistine Goliath. Goliath was insulted that Israel sent out such an unworthy opponent, but he planned to slay the young lad nevertheless. However, David slew Goliath with a slingshot and then cut off the giant's head with his own sword.

The story of young David slaying Goliath got around, and David became an instant hero. This irritated King Saul, because people were praising David instead of him. To make matters worse for Saul, his daughter, Michal, fell in love with David, so David became Saul's son-in-law.

After Saul died, David was anointed king over the people. He had served Saul as a mighty warrior and won many battles for the Hebrew people. He seemed to be an outgoing fellow and well-loved among most of his countrymen. He accomplished many great things as king, including bringing back the Ark of the Covenant.

Many of you may have seen Raiders of the Lost Ark, where the actor Harrison Ford was running around, risking his life to find the ark; well, this is the ark he was looking for. The Ark of the Covenant, made back in the time of Moses, contained the tablets upon which the Ten Commandments were written, as well as other laws given to the people by God. During one of the numerous wars and battles the Hebrew people fought, the ark was lost to an enemy. As an example of just one of his many great accomplishments, David recovered the Ark.

Despite all of the great things he did, one of David's most memorable moments was an enormous sin he com mitted. When he was king, he was out on his patio when he noticed a beautiful woman named Bathsheba down below. He learned that she was the wife of one of his solders, Uriah. There was a war going on, so Uriah was in the field fighting for David.

That did not deter David, so he sent for her, slept with her, and got her pregnant. The problem with politicians running around on their spouses did not start with Bill Clinton; there were hundreds that set the precedence. David wanted to cover his tracks, so he had the commander of the army send Uriah home. When Uriah arrived, David encouraged him to go home and sleep with his wife. Of course, if he were to do this, then all, including Uriah, would think he was the one who got his wife pregnant, not David. However, Uriah did not do this, telling David that his men were staying in tents without their wives and it would be unfair. So David had him over for dinner the next evening and got him drunk on wine and then tried to send him home to his wife, and again, Uriah would not sleep with her but stayed outside.

David then summoned Uriah to take a note back to the commander. It was a sealed note, and it instructed the commander to put Uriah on the front lines in a manner that would ensure his death. Uriah was killed in battle, and David married his wife.

Can you imagine? Remember, David is one of our big heroes. This sorry rascal slept with his solder's wife, tried to cover it up by getting Uriah to sleep with her, and, when that didn't work, had Uriah killed and then married his widow. He makes Bill Clinton look like a choirboy.

I guess David thought he had gotten away with it until God sent the Prophet Nathan to tell David that he knew what he did. Everyone needs someone to hold him or her accountable, and Nathan provided that role for David.

God punished David for what he had done, and David spent a lot of time trying to repent and asking God's forgiveness.

Although God punished David, he also continued to love him and forgave him. David went on to accomplish many other great things, but he also served as a great example of the consequences of our actions on our family, our friends, and our own happiness in life.

One of the things David wanted to do was build a temple in Jerusalem where the people could come to worship God. God told David that he would not allow him to build the temple because he had too much blood on his hands. However, he would allow Solomon, the son of David and the next king, to build the temple.

We are going to expand David's story and talk about his son, Solomon. When Solomon became king, one of the things he prayed for was wisdom. You may have heard the phrase "The wisdom of Solomon," as God granted this wisdom and many riches to boot.

One of the great stories of Solomon's wisdom concerns two women who came to him with a child, each claiming to be the mother. They had come to Solomon for judgment and resolution of the issue. Solomon drew his sword and said he would solve the issue by cutting the baby in two and giving each woman a half. The baby's real mother spoke up and said to give the baby to the other woman. That is how Solomon determined the real mother, and that was pretty clever.

Solomon did build the temple in Jerusalem. This temple was eventually destroyed, and another one was built, and that one was also destroyed. What is now known as the Wailing Wall in Jerusalem is one of the walls of the second temple. Today, Jews and others put prayers in the wall.

Solomon is credited by many for writing three books of the Bible: Song of Songs, Proverbs, and Ecclesiastes.

Song of Songs is one of the most eloquent love poems or sagas one can ever read. In my Sunday school class, one of my favorite people, Lois Rutledge, who is now in her eighties and funny as the dickens, does not see how God would have such a book in the Bible. God may have put that book in there just to irritate Lois. If you ever want to woo your lover, reading Song of Songs to her would be a way.

Proverbs is a book of wise sayings, and Ecclesiastes is a down-to-earth common-sense book on the meaning of life, assuming you have a sense of humor. Many of you that are ex-hippies may identify with Ecclesiastes 3, where Solomon mentions that there is a time for everything, and a 1960s ballad was written: "A time to be born and a time to die, a time to plant and a time to uproot, a time to kill and a time to heal, a time to tear down and a time to build, a time to weep and a time to laugh, a time to mourn and a time to dance" (Ecclesiastes 3:23, niv).

The Bible

One of the ways God reveals himself to us is through his Holy Word, the Bible. It can be a difficult book to read. We discussed some parts of the Bible in earlier chapters. Here is a brief overview.

I have known several folks who all of a sudden want to "get right" with God and get religion. One of their first actions is to get a Bible, start at Genesis, and read it from cover to cover. That is an awful idea. I talked to some poor guy recently and he was in Numbers—ouch! "Art, do you just like to torture yourself?" I asked.

The Old Testament is the first part of the Bible; it consists of thirty-nine books, beginning with Genesis and ending with Malachi. It was mostly written in Hebrew, with some passages in Arabic. The New Testament is the second part of the Bible; it consists of twenty-seven books, beginning with Matthew and ending with Revelation. The New Testament was written mostly in Greek.

I view the Bible as a love story between God and his people—us. It starts out with the creation story in Genesis and quickly gets into the creation of the first man (Adam) and the first woman (Eve). By Genesis 3, Adam and Eve sin by eating fruit from the forbidden tree, and the stage is set. Cain and Abel are introduced by chapter four, where we have the world's first murder. Genesis quickly moves to Noah and the flood, where everyone but Noah, his family, and two each of all creatures drown due to rampant sin.

Genesis is a pretty action-packed book and worth reading. After Noah, we learn about Abraham, his son Isaac, Isaac's sons Jacob and Esau (the answer to many crossword puzzles), and Joseph. At the end of Genesis, many Jewish people are in Egypt, which sets the scene for the exodus.

The book of Exodus is jam-packed with action. It starts with the birth of Moses and the plight of the Jewish people in Egypt. Exodus covers events leading up to the Passover and the exodus from Egypt (hence the name of the book). Once out of Egypt, the Jews wandered in the wilderness for forty years, and the details of this time are documented. It was during this time that God handed Moses the Ten Commandments, which are:

1. Worship only God. Do not put any gods before him.

2. Do not make idols.

3. Do not misuse the name of God. Do not use God's name in vain.

4. Remember the Sabbath and keep it holy. In the early 1990s, I was on a business trip to Israel, which is a Jewish state. On their Sabbath (Friday evening to Saturday evening), they do no work. In my hotel, they had a normal elevator and a "Sabbath" elevator. The Sabbath elevator was preprogrammed to stop on every floor so the Jews would not have to press an elevator button (or do work). Of course, the elevator was slow as molasses. Really smart Jews would get on the normal elevator with a Gentile and ask, "Would you please press floor five?" I guess they figured it was okay for me to meet the wrath of God.

5. Honor your father and your mother.

6. Do not murder.

7. Do not commit adultery.

8. Do not steal.

9. Do not give false testimony against your neighbor.

10. Do not covet your neighbor's stuff.

God handed these to Moses on stone tablets on Mount Sinai.

Many of the Jewish customs and rituals are out lined in Exodus, and most of these traditions continue in the Jewish community today.

The story of Moses picks up again in the book of Deuteronomy, and the story of the forty years of wandering in the desert continues. Also, in Deuteronomy, a successor to Moses, Joshua, is picked.

I always found it interesting that Moses was not allowed to enter the Promised Land, or present-day Israel. Moses had disobeyed God, and that was his punishment. Before Moses died, God allowed him to view the land from a mountain, but Joshua was the one providing the leadership going forward. As great as Moses was, he was also just doing God's work, and it was not about Moses, but about God.

The book after Deuteronomy is named after Joshua, and it is where early life in the Promised Land is discussed. These first books of the Bible get us to the point where the Jews are God's chosen people and they are to be a light unto the rest of the world. They are now in the Promised Land and have developed an organizational structure, rules, and judges. Also during this period of time, the people get disgruntled and complain about all sorts of stuff. Not much has changed in the world, has it?

One of the complaints of the people was that they did not have a king, and all of the nations around them had a king. God was offended by the people's desire for a king; however, he gave them their request. The next several books, ranging from Joshua to 2 Chronicles, discuss the people's plight with their kings. The story of King David is the highlight of these books.

In the middle of the Bible are several books of wisdom and literature. They include Job, Psalms, Proverbs, Ecclesiastes, and Song of Songs. You may have heard people say, "He has the patience of Job." Job was a man who suffered enormous grief but never gave up on God. In the end, he was rewarded richly for his patience.

The next phase of the Old Testament deals with numerous prophets, such as Isaiah and Jeremiah. God still spoke to his people through prophets. There were numerous Jewish kings after David. Some were good, but many were bad. The people seemed to go through cycles. They would start worshiping false idols (remember those Ten Commandments) and doing many other things that irritated God. God would then punish the people, and a good king would show up for a while, and everyone would behave. Then the cycle would repeat.

During one of the bad cycles, God decided to let Israel be conquered and the people be taken into exile in Babylon. You can tell by the tone of many of the books of the Bible whether these books were written before, during, or after the exile to Babylon. It was a big event in the history of the Jewish people, and a significant part of the Old Testament is spent addressing the reasons for the exile and the events after the people's return to Jerusalem. There is a lot of learning and wisdom in those discussions. We then get to the New Testament. The first part of the New Testament is the synoptic Gospels of Matthew, Mark, and Luke. Those are followed by the Gospel of John.

After John is the book of Acts. Acts is the story of the early church after the resurrection of Jesus.

The rest of the New Testament, save Revelation, is letters. Most of the letters are written by the Apostle Paul to the early churches. There are some additional letters written by John, James, Peter, and a few others.

The book of Revelation was written by the Apostle John, sometimes known as John of Patmos, named after the Greek island where the writer was exiled by the Romans for preaching his Christian faith. You may have heard folks talk about the Rapture, the end of the world, and the second coming of Christ.

Most of this comes from the book of Revelation. The bestselling religious series Left Behind was loosely based on Revelation.

Revelation is one of several books in the Bible that is written in an apocalyptic literature style where the author uses symbols to tell the story. In Revelation, it is speculated that the author used symbols that Christians would understand but the Romans would not understand. Revelation is a book that is essentially written in Christian code. Daniel, Zechariah, and Ezekiel are the other books in the Bible written in an apocalyptic style.

The biblical love story starts with creation, tells the story of God's love and our disobedience and a rebellious people, and ends with God reconciling his relationship with his children by sending Jesus Christ to die for our sins. Then God finishes the love story, showing us how to live with him and one another. He ends the love story with his promise to come again and live among us for eternity.

That love story is an all-time best seller. There have been more Bibles sold than any other book in the history of the world.

Who Is Jesus?

Jesus is God incarnate—God in the flesh. He is the long-awaited Messiah.

> In the beginning was the Word, and the Word was with God, and the Word was God. He was with God in the beginning. Through him all things were made; without him nothing was made that has been made. In him was life, and that life was the light of men. The light shines in the darkness but the darkness has not understood it.
>
> John 1:15 (niv)

The Bible is divided into separate books (not chapters) that are put together in a single document. There are two main groupings of all the books, Old Testament and New Testament. The story of Jesus is told in the four books of the Bible's New Testament called the Gospels: Matthew, Mark, Luke, and John. Matthew, Mark, and Luke are referred to as the synoptic Gospels, as they tell their stories in the same order and with many of the same words. The Gospel according to John is probably the most loved book in the Bible by Christians because of its depth and spirituality. John, like Matthew, was one of the twelve disciples of Jesus; he knew Jesus personally.

I would encourage you to start with reading Matthew and Luke, as they are good stories of the life, death, and resurrection of Jesus. I would then read the Gospel of John. In case you are not going to rush out and read the Gospels, I will provide a brief overview.

The life of Jesus begins with a miracle, as his birth mother, Mary, was a virgin. At the time, she was engaged to Joseph. When Joseph learned that his fiancée was pregnant, he was going to discretely divorce her. However, an angel of the Lord appeared to him in a dream and told him that the baby was from the Holy Spirit. This virgin birth was predicted centuries ago in Isaiah 7:14.

The Romans were in charge at the time, and Caesar Augustus had a census taken of the entire Roman world. Everyone had to go to his or her original hometown to register, which for Joseph was Bethlehem, which happened to be the city where King David was anointed by Samuel.

I cannot imagine how poor Mary felt being pregnant, riding all over Israel on a donkey. I bet Joseph did not cross her or leave the toilet seat up. When they finally got to Bethlehem, there was no place to stay, so they ended up staying in a stable, and that is where Jesus was born. Coming to pay homage to the newborn king were shepherds and foreign kings, commonly known as the three wise men. All of the Nativity scenes you see outside of churches during Christmas represent this event and col lection of people. The wise men, who may have been kings or astrologers, brought gifts to baby Jesus, and that is where gift giving at Christmas came from. However, I do not think God intended for us to overindulge and max out our credit cards during this holy day. Several years ago, one of our pastors suggested that we should at least add Jesus to our Christmas giving list each year.

There was another baby born a little earlier than Jesus, and he and Jesus were cousins and would become friends. This baby grew up to be John the Baptizer. John spent his time preaching and telling people to repent. Isaiah 40:35 (niv) predicted such a fellow:

> A voice of one calling: In the desert prepare the way
> for the Lord; make straight in the wilderness a
> highway for our God. Every valley shall be raised
> up, every mountain and hill made low; the rough

ground shall become level the rugged places a plain. And the glory of the Lord will be revealed, and all mankind together will see it. For the mouth of the Lord has spoken.

John the Baptist baptized Jesus:

When all the people were being baptized, Jesus was baptized, too. And as he was praying, heaven was opened and the Holy Spirit descended on him in bodily form like a dove. And a voice came from heaven: "You are my Son, whom I love, with you I am well pleased."

Luke 3:22 (niv)

At this time, Jesus was about to enter his ministry. From the Jordan River, where he was baptized, the Holy Spirit led Jesus to the desert, where he was tempted by the devil for forty days. Numbers mean a lot to Chris tians, and the number forty is an important one. After they escaped from Egypt, the Hebrew people wandered in the desert for forty years before being led to the Promised Land. Twelve is another important number, as Jesus had twelve disciples, there were twelve tribes of Israel, and there are twelve months to a year. Seven is another important one, as it is the biblical number of perfection or completion. The mark of evil, 666, is derived from six being less than perfect, so 666 is bad.

Now back to Jesus being in the desert for forty days. Jesus prevailed over his temptations with the devil and carried out his ministry and ultimate mission. Let's briefly talk about the devil. The devil is a fallen angel, who, like us, had free choice and decided to put his own ego ahead of God. Evil exists in the world, and just as Jesus uses people to carry out good and bring light to the world, the devil uses people to bring evil and darkness into the world. You can't claim that "the devil made me do it!" in an effort to excuse doing something bad. We all have free choice, but we must remember we can be easily tempted by the devil. Christians believe there will be a final show down and that Christ will prevail and we will all live in a heavenly kingdom.

God had several reasons for coming to earth in the form of Jesus.

- To let us know who he is. He did this through the performance of numerous miracles. His first miracle was at a wedding in Canaan, where he turned water to wine. So if you are ever on the TV game show Jeopardy, you will know that "question," if asked. Some other quick ones are walking on water, raising Lazarus from the dead, feeding thousands of people with a few fish and a little bread, and healing many lame and blind people. Jesus did his miracles at various times in front of thousands of people, so we are not just going on hearsay.
- To show us how to live. Over the last several years, people have started wearing plastic bracelets to represent different charities, etc. One of the bracelets has " WWJD" (What Would Jesus Do?) on it. In his ministry, Jesus faced a multitude of situations that we face in everyday life. We have the advantage of seeing how he handled each situation or what he had to say about situations through his many parables (special stories with a message of how to live or understand God).
- To be sacrificed on the cross for our sins. He did this because he loves us immensely and wants to reconcile our relationship with him.

Jesus was Jewish and part of God's chosen people, the Hebrews. Being chosen didn't necessarily mean being better than anyone else in the world. In fact, Jewish life and history have been tough. They were chosen to be God's example of how God wants to relate to all of us in the good times and bad. God told us that the Messiah would come from the line of King David, and Jesus's genealogy can be traced back to King David. Many of the Jews just didn't get it when Jesus came on earth and rose from the dead. They are still looking for the Messiah. So being chosen isn't like being the teacher's pet.

One of the major reasons God came to earth in the form of Jesus is to show us how to live. A lot of this he did by the telling of parables, and we will hit upon some of the most famous. The parable of the Good Samaritan is a classic. Imagine the scene with Jesus teaching and one of the priests trying to trip him up. Here is how Luke relates the story.

> On one occasion an expert in the law stood up to test Jesus. "Teacher," he asked, "what must I do to inherit eternal life?" "What is written in the Law?" Jesus replied. "How do you read it?" He answered: "Love the Lord your God with all your heart and with all your soul and with all your strength and with all your mind" and "Love your neighbor as yourself." "You have answered correctly," Jesus replied. "Do this and you will live." But he wanted to justify himself, so he asked Jesus, "And who is my neighbor?" In reply Jesus said, "A man was going down from Jerusalem to Jericho, when he fell into the hands of robbers. They stripped him of his clothes, beat him and went away, leaving him half dead. A priest happened to be going down the same road, and when he came to the place and saw him, passed on the other side So too, a Levite, when he came to the place and saw him, passed by on the other side. But a Samaritan, as he traveled, came where the man was; and when he saw him he took pity on him. He went to him and bandaged his wounds, pouring on oil and wine. Then he put the man on his own donkey. Took him to an inn and took care of him. The next day he took out two silver coins and gave them to the innkeeper. "Look after him," he said, "and when I return, I will reimburse you for any extra expense you may have." Which of these do you think was a neighbor to the man who fell into the hands of robbers?" The expert in the law replied, "The one who had mercy on him." Jesus told him, "Go and do likewise."
>
> Luke 10:25-37 (niv)

Some tidbits that make this parable even more meaningful are priests and Levites were highly regarded among the Hebrew people, and Samaritans were looked down upon. The roles that Jesus had them play in the parable made the story more powerful.

What Is "the Church?"

I co-lead an employment networking group at our church that meets every Monday morning. It is a group that helps those who are unemployed find a job. Most people that come to the group are not members of our church or any church. One Monday, a new man came, and during his story of his employment issues, he started talking about religion and about people claiming to being "born again." He had some derogatory things to say about the subject, and several others gave "knowing nods" of agreement. It was a damning indictment of the church and those who are members. Sean Wise, the other co-leader, and I sat quietly, as it was not the time and place to argue.

People are not born with information; somehow, they have to obtain it. When I see how the church is portrayed by the media (whose members are mostly unchurched) and by television in general, it is no wonder that there is a negative perception among those who do not go to church. Also, these negative portrayals provide a handy excuse for not going to church.

The church itself needs to accept responsibility for priests who abuse children, for national religious leaders who commit adultery (and condemn others that do), for ignoring injustice at times, and for making some visitors feel unwelcome. You know why the church is so awful sometimes? Because it is made up of people, and people screw up! They screw up just like Adam, Eve, and you and me. So if you are going to condemn the church, go ahead and condemn every organization that is made up of human beings, because all human beings will fall short of your expectations. We most certainly fall short of God's expectations.

In 2010, there was an awful earthquake in Haiti, followed by one in Chile. One of the stories the news media hyped was about some missionaries who had allegedly taken advantage of orphans. The story later was proven to be false, and the missionaries were actually helping the orphans. However, the main story should have been, "What are all those church people doing there?" Years after Hurricane Katrina hit the Gulf Coast, teams from the United Methodist Church traveled to Mississippi and Louisiana to repair and rebuild homes of people they didn't even know. I cannot recall a time in my lifetime when there was a disaster anywhere in the world where American Christians were not actively involved in helping both financially and with direct hands-on work relieving pain and suffering and expecting absolutely nothing in return—not even recognition. In today's unemployment crisis, I see where many who had never used food pantries are using them. Where do you think the food comes from? It comes from the church.

Our church had another mission team return from the Mississippi Gulf Coast, where it was supporting Katrina relief. It has been four years since that devastating hurricane hit shore. The United Methodist Church has already sent a hundred and sixty thousand people and supplied over a hundred million dollars' worth of labor and another hundred million dollars in materials for relief to this region. Plans are to continue this effort.

The church has done so much good in the community and in the world for so long that we just take it for granted. Christ does his work in the world through people and through his church.

The church is the body of Christ, and like Christ, it is persecuted and abused by many, especially those who are ignorant.

Jesus had many followers, but there were twelve men who were in his "inner circle": his twelve disciples. They were:

1. Peter. Peter is probably the most famous of the disciples, and he seemed to have an outgoing personality. Peter is the one whom Christ said was the rock upon which he would build his church, and Roman Catholics consider him to be the first pope.

Peter had a vision from God that led to non-Jewish being included into the Christian Church without having to follow Jewish customs. Peter, who was also crucified, insisted on being crucified upside down so he would not dishonor Christ. I never understood that thinking, but it fits Peter's personality.

2. Andrew was Peter's brother and, like Peter, a fisherman. Jesus told them that they would become "fishers of men."

3. James, son of Zebedee.

4. John. He was the brother of James and writer of the Gospel of John. Many feel that he was also the writer of the book of Revelation.

5. Philip.

6. Bartholomew.

7. Thomas. Thomas's claim to fame was his questioning of the resurrection of Jesus, even after many testified to having seen Jesus. Thomas said he could not believe it unless he saw Jesus and put his hands into his wounds. When Christ appeared to Thomas, he finally believed in the resurrection, but he inspired the term "Doubting Thomas."

8. Matthew. The writer of the Gospel of Matthew.

9. James, son of Alpheus.

10. Thaddeus.

11. Simon the Zealot.

12. Judas Iscariot. Judas is the one who betrayed Christ and turned him over to the chief priest. Judas received thirty pieces of silver to betray Jesus. After Jesus was convicted, Judas threw the money into the temple and hanged himself in remorse.

Jesus had a last meal with his disciples (the Last Supper), and it was held in what is now known as "the upper room," which is in Jerusalem. One of my preachers told a funny story concerning the upper room. The Upper Room is the name of a daily devotional run by the United Methodist Church and is located in Nashville, Tennessee. The Upper Room has a nice chapel, museum, and a beautiful carving of Jesus and his disciples sitting at the table during the Last Supper. The preacher was relating a story of an elderly group of American tourists in Israel. When the group's tour bus stopped at the real upper room, the bus emptied out, except one elderly couple. When the driver asked if they were going to exit the bus, they said, "No, we have seen the real Upper Room in Nashville, so there is no need to see this one." I am sure that tickled the folks in Nashville.

Jesus had a frank discussion with his disciples during the Last Supper, which, again, was a Seder meal. He told them he must suffer, and Peter promised Jesus he also would suffer along with him. "But he replied, Lord, I am ready to go with you to prison and to death" (Luke 22:33, niv).

However, Jesus knew that his disciples, including Peter, would abandon him. "Jesus answered, I tell you, Peter, before the rooster crows today, you will deny three times that you know me" (Luke 22:34, niv).

Later that evening, Jesus went to the Mount of Olives to pray, and some of his disciples remained nearby. It was there that Judas led the chief priest to Jesus, and they took him away. During the interrogation, beatings, and abuse Jesus suffered, his disciples left him, and Peter three times denied knowing him. After Peter had denied him that third time and the rooster crowed, Peter and Jesus made eye contact, and Peter wept. Peter was human and, like us, had weak moments. Jesus later used Peter to help organize and lead the initial church.

Jesus did not have any additional contact with his disciples and followers until his resurrection three days later on what is now called Easter Sunday.

Where did the church come from? Let us go back to our friends walking to Emmaus. The time following the death and resurrection of Christ was stressful for his followers. Our two friends walking to Emmaus with Jesus were approaching the village, which was their destination. They urged Jesus, whom they still did not recognize, to go with them, so Jesus went to stay with them.

> When he was at the table with them, he took bread, gave thanks, broke it, and began to give it to them. Then their eyes were opened and they recognized him, and he disappeared from their sight. The asked each other, "Were not our hearts burning within us while he talked with us on the road and opened the Scriptures to us?" They got up and returned at once to Jerusalem. There they found the Eleven and those with them, assembled together and saying, "It is true! The Lord has risen and has appeared to Simon." Then the two told what had happened on the way and how Jesus was recognized by them when he took the bread.
>
> Luke 24:30-35 (niv)

Jesus was with the disciples for over forty days (there is that number again) after his resurrection, and he instructed them on what they should do when he ascended into heaven. As you can imagine, they had lots of questions.

> So when they met together, they asked him, "Lord, are you at this time going to restore the kingdom to Israel?" He said to them, "It is not for you to know the times or dates the Father has set by his own authority. But you will receive power when the Holy Spirit comes on you, and you will be my witnesses in Jerusalem and all Judea and Samaria, and to the ends of the earth."
>
> Acts 1:68 (niv)

After that, Jesus ascended into heaven. One of their first acts was to replace Judas with Matthias as the twelfth disciple.

Imagine how his followers felt. Their Lord had been abused and crucified by the Romans at the will of the chief priests. They were scared. The high priests were on a roll, and having followers of Christ tortured and executed would be a natural thing for them to do.

The story of the church begins in the book of Acts, which was written by Luke, who also wrote the Gospel that bears his name.

The event that would be remembered as the beginning of the church was the coming of the Holy Spirit, as Jesus had promised his followers. It came during what is known as Pentecost. You may have heard of Pentecostal churches; well, this is where they got their name.

> When the day of Pentecost came, they were all together in one place. Suddenly a sound like the blowing of a violent wind came from heaven and filled the whole house where they were sitting. They saw what seemed to be tongues of fire that separated and came to rest on each of them. All of them were filled with the Holy Spirit and began to speak in other tongues as the Spirit enabled them.
>
> Acts 2:14 (niv)

You may have heard of people claiming to speak in tongues. I have seen this before, and I do not know what to think. Those few times when I heard someone speaking in tongues, there was an interpreter. In some Protestant denominations, especially Pentecostal, you are looked down upon if you have not had an experience speaking in tongues. I mention this only for information purposes, not as judgment. The global body of Christ is made up of many different viewpoints and talents. I am confident that God has his reason for this, although it would be nice if they all agreed with me (ha). These people were acting so crazy on Pentecost that many of the observers thought they were drunk. Believe me; if you have ever seen any one speak in tongues, you are also going to drag out the breathalyzer.

Peter then began to earn his keep after having denied Christ. Acts 2 describes how Peter addressed the crowd and explained that the people were not drunk—it was only nine in the morning. He explained to the crowd of Jews that the Prophet Joel had said that God would pour out his Holy Spirit on the people, and he went on to preach perhaps the first Christian sermon after the resurrection of Christ. After his sermon, many of the Jews wanted to know what they should do.

> Peter replied, "Repent and be baptized, every one of you, in the name of Jesus Christ for the forgiveness of your sins. And you will receive the gift of the Holy Spirit. The promise is for you and your children and for all who are far off—for all whom the Lord our God will call." With many other words he warned them; and he pleaded with them, "Save yourselves from this corrupt generation." Those who accepted his message were baptized, and about three thousand were added to their numbers that day.
>
> Acts 2:38-41 (niv)

Did you get that? Three thousand folks joined the church that day, and the church—the body of Christ— was born. I doubt there were too many Romans that joined, so the vast majority of these new Christians were Jewish, like the apostles (the twelve disciples) and Christ. I want to stop here and talk a little about Christian Jewish relations. For too many years, some Christians were hostile to Jews, and they rationalized their actions by saying, "The Jews murdered Jesus." What were they thinking? Jesus was Jewish; the first Christian Church was made up of all Jews with Jewish leadership. The outcome of this bias was that many Christians abandoned many of the Jewish traditions that were inspired by God and are holy moments. Anti-Semitism, supported by the church, evolved over the ages and crested in Europe during World War II, with German Nazis leading the Holocaust. It was a sad era in the history of the church, which again is made up of sinful people, like you and me.

There are numerous major events in the history of the church. One major event is when the Roman emperor Constantine, legalized Christianity and used it as his foundation to build a new Rome. This was the beginning of what we now know as the Roman Catholic Church. The term Catholic means "universal," so you will hear that read in the Apostles' Creed, which is read in both Roman Catholic and Protestant churches. One of the kings of England had a problem with the Roman Catholic Church over their stance on divorce, because the king wanted to divorce a wife. From that point, the Church of England was created, and hence the beginning of part of the Protestant movement. Also, Martin Luther felt there was enormous corruption in the church, so he also broke away from the mainline Roman Catholic.

Today, there are probably hundreds of different denominations throughout the world, each having a different twist or an ethnic slant to their belief.

The most rigid of the denominations are probably the Amish, Quakers, Mennonites, and other Germanic groups that practice a plain existence. All of those groups were persecuted during our World Wars because they refused to go to war and fight. Years ago, our company did business with an Ohio firm, Sauder Furniture, which was founded and run by Mennonites. Our main contact in the firm told about how one of his uncles was nearly hanged during World War II, and they did go as far as to strip his shirt and paint a yellow streak down his back.

Today, churches range from liberal institutions, such as the Unitarian, to rigid and conservative groups, such as the Pentecostals and Baptists, and include everything in between. In the United Methodist Church, we have members who are liberal, conservative, and in between. I guess the point is that if you want to worship God, you should not have a hard time finding a bunch of people who believe as you do.

One of the things we take for granted in the United States is our freedom of religion. In many countries, such as those that are Islamic states, one does not have the freedom to worship God unless they are Muslim. Socialist and communist governments have also restricted freedom of religion.

Who is Paul?

Have you ever heard someone utter the phrase "I had a Damascus Road experience?" That comes from the Apostle Paul, who is one of the more interesting characters in our Bible. Of all people, Paul is the best example of how God uses someone for his purpose.

From what we know, Paul was a Roman citizen, a Jew, well educated, and probably divorced or widowed. In the early stages of the church, he was one of the Jews who was adamant that the Christian Church was wrong and that those who embraced it should be punished. Paul was present when Stephen, the first Christian martyr, was stoned to death. Paul went through a name change. He was first referred to as Saul, and then Paul, so I will use both names as we weave back and forth. Saul is inherently a Jewish name, and Paul is more Gentile. As Paul ministered to the Gentiles, it would be appropriate for him to have a Gentile name.

> Meanwhile, Saul was still breathing out murderous threats against the Lord's disciples. He went to the high priest and asked him for letters to the synagogues in Damascus, so that if he found any there who belonged to the Way [Christians], whether men or women, he might take them as prisoners to Jerusalem. As he neared Damascus on his journey, suddenly a light from heaven flashed around him. He fell to the ground and heard a voice say to him, "Saul, Saul, why do you persecute me?" "Who are you Lord?" Saul asked. "I am Jesus, whom you are

persecuting," he replied. "Now get up and go into the city, and you will be told what you must do."

Acts 9:16 (niv)

When Saul tried to get up, he discovered he was blind. Saul (soon to be Paul) just had a personal encounter with Jesus. Then Jesus spoke to Ananias, a Christian in Damascus, about helping Paul. Ananias did not want to help Saul, because he was aware of Saul's reputation.

> "Lord," Ananias answered, "I have heard many reports about this man and all the harm he has done to your saints in Jerusalem. And he has come here with authority from the chief priests to arrest all who call on your name." But the Lord said to Ananias, "Go! This man is my chosen instrument to carry my name before the Gentiles and their kings and before the people of Israel. I will show him how much he must suffer for my name."

Acts 9:13-16 (niv)

Being Jewish gives Saul credibility with some Jews, and he certainly knows their viewpoint. Being a Roman citizen is a huge advantage in the world in which he lived. A Roman citizen had many privileges that other people did not have. Paul seemed to be a perfect fit for this role Jesus had for him.

What if Saul had said no? Do you think that would have been it and God would have just given up? I don't think so. God would have just chosen someone else. However, he certainly put the heat on Saul. Getting struck blind is an attention getter. I imagine it would have been pretty tough to say no. I asked that question for your and my benefit. God has work planned for us also, and we can say yes or no. God's work is going to get done anyway.

Paul traveled throughout the Gentile world and wrote much of what we call the New Testament, and many of the books are named after the places and people he visited, such as Romans, Corinthians, Ephesians, Galatians, and Philippians.

He was a controversial fellow when he was alive and, even to this day, stirs a lot of emotion in many Christians.

This is a big moment in the evolution of God's love story with us. Remember when we talked about how God had his chosen people, the Jews? Most of God's work up to this point has had the Jewish people as the focus. Now Jesus has anointed someone to minister and carry God's word to the Gentiles, all of those who are not Jewish.

How About This Sin Thing? Am I Going to Hell?

I like to train dogs as a hobby, and I am eager to learn as much as I can. One thing I have discovered through reading, lectures, and personal experience is that dogs respond better to positive training than to negative. One trainer told me his motto was "Fair, Fun, and Firm," which means the dog must know what you want it to do when you give a command; training and being with you should be fun; and you must be firm—when a dog understands the command, it must obey the command.

Dogs that win obedience trials today are much more adept than years ago when trainers used mostly negative reinforcement (the yank and jerk method). If my dog is anxious to do something because of the reward and fun associated with it, then she is much more likely to do it with ease. Having said that, there is still the occasion for what we call a "hard correction" with a dog. On minor stuff like fixing to get into something, I use a simple "nope" with Maggie, and if she doesn't respond, then there comes a sterner "no." However, for really bad behavior or just ignoring a command, I will give a hard correction, which is a "no," followed by grabbing her by the nape of her neck (like her mother did) and shaking. Now that she is older, I cannot remember the last time I gave Maggie a hard correction, as she seems to want to learn and try and do what is right, although we still have our "nopes" on a routine basis.

In giving instruction to others on how to have a relationship with God, I embrace the same model used by successful dog trainers. That is, positive is better than negative. I have heard it said that good preaching ought to comfort the afflicted and afflict those that are comfortable. I do not think any church gets it perfect when treating and reacting to their members with respect to doing the "right thing."

Some more conservative churches talk a lot about sin and repentance. In these churches, some people can get the feeling that they can do nothing right to please God, and they are made to feel small and bad. That is not what God intended. Other churches just think everything and all behavior is fine and dandy. Well, everything isn't fine and dandy, as we all mess up and fall short of what God wants us to do, and we all need a correction—at least the occasional "nope" correction. We should not need a "no" and a shake of the nape of the neck every week.

What does God have to say about all of this? I have often referred to the Bible as a love story about God and his people. Throughout time, God has given some "hard corrections"—for example, when he flooded the world and everyone died, except for Noah, his family, and the animals in the ark. Unfortunately, that is where some dogmatic churches seem to stop reading the love story. Jesus also said that one must forgive seventy times seventy and said to love your neighbor as yourself. If you have children and you love your children, then you have a small glimmer of how God loves you. He loves you a lot more than you love your children, although that may be hard for you to imagine. So do you really believe that God intends for you to get a hard correction every time you go to church or attend a worship service? No, he doesn't.

Your children do not have to earn your love, nor do you have to earn God's love. God wants good things for you; the only variable is you. The theologians talk about the different levels of God's grace. Here is my basic understanding of grace:

1. God loves each of us when we are still in our mother's womb. We know nothing of God, and he loves us.
2. There comes a time when we are aware there is a God. Either Mom or Dad tells us that there is a God or somewhere along the line we get that information. Let's say you understand that there is a God and accept the fact that it is true but it remains a "so what?" to you. God still loves you and is waiting for you to engage him.
3. There are those who strive to be disciples and endeavor to enhance their relationship with Christ, and he loves them but not any more than the other categories of grace. In my opinion, if you are involved with God and his work, then you just have a more meaningful life. Perhaps you get to experience a bit of heaven on earth.

Many churches and perhaps religions put the cart before the horse. That is when someone new comes to church, and all the talk is about sin and everything the poor person is doing wrong. If instead churches can provide an environment in which that person is encouraged to grow his or her relationship with God, the sin issue can be worked out between God and that person. When we truly love someone, we want to please them. When we fail to please them or, worse yet, hurt them, we should feel bad. So it should be with our relationship with God.

That does not mean the church should never talk about sin and hold people accountable. Some churches overdo it. We all need people who will hold us account able, and we need to hold ourselves accountable.

In summary, we all do bad stuff, even Billy Graham and Mother Teresa. When you take a look at the Ten Commandments and all of the other stuff we are supposed to do, there is no way any one person is going to get all of that right. We all have fits of selfish anger and have thoughts we shouldn't have. Only Jesus Christ lived a perfect life. The good news is that Jesus died for our sins, and God's promise is that those who believe in him will have everlasting life. That works for me.

Also, there is no pecking order as to whom God loves the most or who is held in highest esteem. Here is a cool parable that Jesus told from Matthew 20:

> For the kingdom of heaven is like a landowner who went out early in the morning to hire men to work in his vineyard. He agreed to pay them a denarius for the day and sent them into his vineyard. About the third hour he went out and saw others standing in the marketplace doing nothing. He told them, "You also go and work in my vineyard and I will pay you whatever is right." So they went. He went out again about the sixth hour and the ninth hour and did the same thing. About the eleventh hour he went out and found still others standing around. He asked them, "Why have you been standing here all day long doing nothing?" "Because no one has hired us," they answered. He said to them, "You also go and work in my vineyard." When evening came, the owner of the vineyard said to his foreman, "Call the workers and pay them their wages, beginning with the last ones hired and going on to the first." The workers who were hired about the eleventh hour came and each received a denarius. So when those came who were hired first, they expected to receive more. But each one of them also received a denarius. When they received it, they began to grumble against the landowner. "These men who were hired last worked only one hour," they said, "and you have made them equal to us who have borne the burden of the work and the heat of the day." But he answered one of them, "Friend, I am not being unfair to you. Didn't you agree to work for a denarius? Take your pay and go. I want to give the man who was hired last the same as I gave you. Don't I have the right to do what I want with my own money? Or are you envious

because I am generous?" So the last will be first and the first will be last."

Mathew 20: 1-16 (niv)

Several years ago, I was on a walk with a young man I mentored. He was a devout Christian and really struggled with this parable. He basically said, "Why should people who have been bad and sorry all their life get the same benefit with God as I do? I have been good for many years." Well, that is just the way it is. God loves us all the same, and the gifts of eternal life are the same for all, regardless of when you make the decision to come to Christ. That forgiven death row inmate being led to his execution is in just as good a shape as Reverend Graham and Mother Teresa. However, Reverend Graham and Mother Teresa had a lot more fun and enjoyment on earth.

Let me offer a word of caution. Not that anyone would do this, but having a strategy of doing whatever the heck you want until you see the train bearing down on you and then all of a sudden getting a dose of religion is not going to work. People do not "get religion." What they get is a relationship with Christ, which is no different than any other relationship; you have to put out some effort to make it work. God sees a person's heart and knows true confession and faith over just saving your skin in eternity after a lifetime of selfish, lustful, and criminal living.

If you are aware that there is a God and you choose (remember that freedom of choice thing) to ignore or mock God, then you might just go to hell when you die. I don't know about you, but I am going to put my faith in God and not in some intellectual bozo that wants to say belief in God is nothing more than superstition.

Are you or are you not going to hell? I don't know. Eternity is one heck of a long time compared to the brief eighty years of being good here on earth, so my advice is to try and stack the odds in your favor of not going to hell. We have all probably heard stories of folks that died momentarily and came back claiming they had seen heaven or some pretty cool things. There are also some folks that have died momentarily and claim they have been to hell. One such fellow is Bill Wiese, who wrote the best seller 23 Minutes in Hell. He doesn't claim that he died, but God sent him to hell for a peek so he could tell others about the experience. As the title reflects, he claims to have spent twenty-three minutes in hell, and from his description, it is scary—not a place one wants to spend any time, much less the remainder of time.

Jesus said that the way to the Father is through him. Does Jesus give you a second chance after you croak? Again, I don't know. I have many Jewish friends. What is going to happen to them when they die? Does God cut them some slack because of his history with them, and again, is there some sort of a staging area where folks learn the truth? Guess that is something to look forward to.

What Do I Do with This Information?

Ilene came into our employment networking group late, no makeup, and looking sort of ragged. I sensed when she took her seat that it was going to be a bad morning with her, as she has highs and lows, and things were not going well. She had been unemployed for eight months, had not made her mortgage payment in six months, and the promising job opportunities she had just two weeks before had fallen through. She was crying and nearly out of control because she did not know what to do. Two other women chimed in, saying they knew her pain and were in the same boat. They were all single, in their fifties, had been unemployed for a long time, and financial pressure was at a maximum.

One of the ladies was adamantly unchurched. One seemed to believe in God but was uninvolved with God. Carol, on the other hand, was just as desperate but seemed to be calmer and offered a witness. She said that several weeks ago, she finally "let go and left it to God." She went on to say how she immediately felt an overall peace and that things were going better. The other two women were so absorbed in their problems that they did not hear Carol. Ilene spoke at length about the "things" she was about to lose. Yes, it is horrible, but I thought that she still had her health and many other things to be thankful for.

The next morning I was reading a devotional from the upper room, and the scripture was one of my favorites; it addresses worry.

> Therefore I tell you, do not worry about your life, what you will eat or drink; or about your body, what you will wear. Is not life more important than food, and the body more important than clothes? Look at the birds of the air; they do not sow or reap or store away in barns, and yet your heavenly Father feeds them. Are you not much more valuable than they? Who of you by worrying can add a single hour to his life? And why do you worry about clothes? See how the lilies of the field grow. They do not labor or spin. Yet I tell you that not even Solomon in all his splendor was dressed like one of these. If that is how God clothes the grass of the field, which is here today and tomorrow is thrown into the fire, will he not much more clothe you, O you of little faith? So do not worry, saying, What shall we eat? Or What shall we drink? Or What shall we wear? For the pagans run after all these things, and your heavenly Father knows that you need them. But seek first his kingdom and his righteousness, and all these things will be given to you as well. Therefore do not worry about tomorrow, for tomorrow will worry about itself. Each day has enough trouble of its own.
> Matthew 6:25-34 (niv)

It could be the scripture of those who, like me, run a small business. I had a successful industrial career and moved up the corporate ladder quickly. I was a vice president of operations for a midsized paint company before I was thirty-five, and by the time I was thirty-seven, I was running the world's largest paint factory for Sherwin Williams. I thought I was the stuff. I got fired at age forty, which was a new experience for me. I had another job offer in the paint industry, making more money than I was at Sherwin-Williams and doing about the same thing, fixing their manufacturing operations. Although I was still young, I was bored of doing the same thing all over again. I wanted a new challenge, and I had always wanted to start my own business. What better time to start? I got a book on starting a business that suggested you have three years' annual salary saved before embarking on such a journey. We did not have this kind of money, so I rationalized that such a recommendation was probably for people not as bright as I who wanted to start a business. So I went down into the basement, got a business line installed, had some business cards printed, and off I went to make my fortunes. In about eighteen months, Linda and I had plowed through every dime we had. I had used all our retirement, all our credit cards were maxed out, and I did not know where the next house payment was coming from. The IRS owed me a sum of money that would have paid the mortgage; however, they are inept, and them paying us the money they owed in a timely manner was out of the question. I can remember holding Linda in my arms because she was scared. She wanted reassurance that all would be well.

By this time, I had already begun to attend church again and had put legitimate effort into my relationship with Jesus. On the basement's hard concrete floor, I got down on my knees and put the problem in God's lap. My prayer was something to the effect of: "Lord, if you do not want me to do this consulting thing, fine; find something else for me to do. However, if you want me to continue down this path, I need some help."

The next day, Georgia Pacific called with seven thousand dollars' worth of work. That seven thousand dollars was going to be enough to keep the wolf off the door for several months. At the time, I was taking a Bible course called Disciple I. When the seven-thousand-dollar check arrived, we were studying the lesson on tithing. My next prayer was, "Father, you are kidding! You want me to write you a check for seven hundred dollars?" The answer was something to the effect of, "Yep." That was over two decades ago, and our company continues to tithe to this day.

For me, letting go and letting God also gave me a sense of peace, and whenever I am disciplined to do that, I am much more at peace. I wish I could snap my fingers and Ilene, Teresa, and others would have that peace.

Many of us feel secure with our friends and family. When I am with my wife and daughter, I feel special. They know me pretty well and accept me with all of my warts and defects. In my tough times, they are there. A relationship with Christ is like a family relationship on steroids. Christ knows me better than Linda and Leigh, and he loves me more. He also is the same for both of them, so with Christ in the picture, the whole family and individual being is stronger and better equipped to endure life's challenges.

My wife has an aunt who is one of the unhappiest people I know. She is currently in her eighties and bitter about everything. She has nothing nice to say about anyone and seems to have one heartache after another, most of which are self-inflicted. I compare her to eighty-year old people in my church congregation. There is simply no comparison. Those folks are full of life. Do they have problems like Linda's aunt? Of course they do—many of them have worse problems. However, they have a relationship with God and a community of believers that love them. They look better, act better, and contribute more to the world than Linda's aunt.

So what do you do with this information? We have adequately discussed the personality and being of God. The variable in all of this is us. What are we doing here? Each of us is here to do God's will, and that is how we experience the most out of life. If you believe in God but have been away from God or the church for years or decades, you are not alone. Most active Christians that I know have at one time in their lives drifted away from God. As I mentioned before, God loves you as much as anyone, but you will not get the most out of life sitting on the bench. All of us "make a difference." I have many neighbors who are wonderful folks, and they make a positive difference in the lives of their fellow man. They will get even more out of life by involving God in their activities. Here are some thoughts if you want to pick up the pace with your relationship with God.

1. Find a church you are comfortable with. Visit the worship services, introduce yourself to the pastors, find a friend who attends, and join some of their activities, such as charity and mission work.

2. Spend time with God each day—meditate and pray. Pray for guidance on what God wants for you to do, how to handle the next project you have, how to be a good spouse, parent, and friend. Also, pray not to be afraid, for help and healing of others, and to thank God for specific blessings over the last twenty-four hours. Many get a daily devotional to help them along. The Upper Room and Daily Bread are two popular ones. You may want to ask a friend what they use. During your time with God each day, pray—talk to God. Learn to pray during routine endeavors, such as driving, taking a walk, or washing the dishes.

3. Once you join a church (or even beforehand), get involved in a small study group. A healthy, small group does a lot more than just study, as they support one another and become like a second family. They will lift you up in prayer, offer advice, and love you unconditionally.

4. Eventually, take a Bible class that leads you through the entire Bible or at least the majority in sequence. Many believers go their entire life and study certain chapters but never put the entire Bible together. It is a book that needs to be seen in its entirety, along with the study of individual chapters, people, eras, or themes.

5. Find out about your spiritual gifts. Each of us has been given special gifts by the Holy Spirit. Work with some folks to discern yours.

6. If you have not already done so, participate in the sacraments. If you have not been baptized, go ahead and do so.
7. Go out and help others in the name of Christ. You will more than likely get more joy than those you are helping. Some of my most memorable experiences in life have been working with other Christians to make things better for others.

You should develop a network of spiritual friends that can help you in your journey. I wish I could say go see any pastor and that pastor would be a disciple and be able to help guide you. That is simply not the case. We have had five pastors since I have been a member of our church. I would consider two of them to be disciples and three non-disciples.

How can you tell who would be a good spiritual leader or not? The Bible tells us that you can judge a tree by the fruit it bears. The Bible also spells out the "fruits of the Spirit," which are love, joy, peace, patience, kindness, good ness, fruitfulness, gentleness, and self-control. If you find someone who is perfect in all those areas, you have stumbled upon the risen Lord, as there is no one who is going to nail those perfectly. However, I am sure you know some people whose behavior is in alignment with those traits. I would start with that person and ask their advice.

Summary

The previous chapter asked what are you going to do with any new information you may have obtained. This summary chapter will ask if are you going to do anything.

You may have read this and nothing will change for you. Perhaps you are "church damaged" or you are angry with God or just feel you do not want to be bothered. What then will make you happy and give you fulfillment? I hope you will not be casting your lot with some individual, other people, a sports team, or your own good looks and talent. If so, disappointment will be your shadow in the long run. It is just a matter of time.

One of my favorite parables is the Parable of the Sower, which is in all three synoptic Gospels. I like the one from Luke 8. Jesus had been traveling from town to town preaching, and he told the following story:

> A farmer went out to sow his seed. As he was scattering the seed, some fell along the path; it was trampled on, and the birds of the air ate it up. Some fell on rock, and when it came up, the plants withered because they had no moisture. Other seed fell among thorns, which grew up with it and choked the plants. Still other seed fell on good soil. It came up and yielded a crop, a hundred times more than was sown.
>
> Luke 8:58a (niv)

When his disciples asked him what the parable meant, Jesus replied:

> This is the meaning of the parable: The seed is the word of God. Those along the path are the ones who hear, and then the devil comes and takes away the word from their hearts, so that they may not believe and be saved. Those on the rock are the ones who receive the word with joy when they hear it, but they have no root. They believe for a while, but in the time of testing they fall away. The seed that fell among thorns stands for those who hear, but as they go on their way they are choked by life's worries, riches and pleasures, and they do not mature. But the seed on good soil stands for those with a noble and good heart, who hear the word, retain it, and by persevering produce a crop.
>
> Luke 8:11-15 (niv)

Each year, our church has a garage sale to raise money for missions. It is a huge event, where we raise nearly twenty thousand dollars. Those of you that have had neighborhood garage sales probably find it hard to imagine one that raises that kind of revenue. After everything is picked through and sold, we give the rest to charities, and those charities schedule trucks in advance to come pick up the merchandise. I was toting material out to one of the trucks and got into a conversation with the truck driver. He told me a tale of woe. He was living with his girlfriend, and she had given them a child. She was kicking him out of their apartment because she had found another boyfriend. There were also drugs and alcohol involved. I played the role of a good listener as this young man continued to tell me one problem after another. Many, if not all, of his problems were self-inflicted. I thought about that poor child being raised in that environment. I quietly asked myself why he was telling me all this. Soon, our brief encounter came to an end, as he had to finish loading the truck, and I felt I needed to go haul more merchandise around. He left, and I am certain I will never see him again.

I blew it. This young man was at a church and, for whatever reason, was reaching out to me. I gave him nothing other than a word of encouragement concerning his job. What could I have done or said? I knew what the young man needed, but I did not know what to do. I choked.

I asked our pastor, Jim Farmer, what I should have done. Jim suggested that I should have asked him how life was working for him. If he told me that it was not working well, then perhaps I should ask him if he were interested in trying a different lifestyle. If his answer was yes, then he embarks on a life plan outlined in chapter eleven. Finding and embracing your God-given purpose in life (the answer to "What am I doing here?") is not difficult, but it is different. It is not difficult because God is with us, even when our mind is not in the right place or we err. It is different because God replaces whatever focus you previously had in life. The spiritual practices outlined in chapter eleven are different than what one might be doing today. If you want to dig deeper into what God has in store for you, I would suggest reading *The Purpose Driven Life* by Rick Warren.

I hope you enjoyed this book and it answered some questions for you. I pray that each one reading this will have the peace of God in their heart and be blessed.

www.ingramcontent.com/pod-product-compliance
Lightning Source LLC
Chambersburg PA
CBHW060136050426

42448CB00010B/2163